*India's Cuisine—Delicious and Healthy
from the kitchen of
Shuma Chakravarty*

"Shuma Chakravarty's book guides readers in the preparation of authentic Indian cuisine. She transports the American reader into the heart of the Indian village. In that village, modern, commercial clichés are pared away and Indian spices like cumin, coriander and turmeric take center stage. Her recipes are detailed and real."
-Ashish Chopra,
The Maharaja Restaurant, Cambridge, MA

ISBN: 978-0-9858282-4-0
Copyright © Shuma Chakravarty 2013

Published by:
CONVERPAGE
23 Acorn Street
Scituate, MA 02066
www.converpage.com

ACKNOWLEDGEMENTS

I wish to thank Pamela McCallum, my publisher. I wish to thank Craig Smith for his technical assistance, editorial expertise and exemplary patience. I wish to thank Jill Christensen of Montana for her generous friendship and moral support for many years. I wish to thank Mr. Ashish Chopra for his description of my book. I wish to thank Margaret Studier, Managing Editor of *Harvard Theological Review*, for her generous friendship and moral support for many years. She often treats me to delicious meals at the Maharaja Restaurant in Cambridge, MA.

I wish to thank Laura Whitney, Librarian of the *Harvard Divinity School Library*, for her moral support of my altruism and appreciation of my scholarly work. I wish to thank computer scientist Prentiss Knowlton of CA for his appreciation of my books and essays. I wish to thank Professor John Burt of Brandeis University for his moral support and friendship. I have enjoyed eating Indian meals with him at the Maharaja Restaurant in Cambridge, MA. I wish to thank Bill/Birendra (my " Mr. W. H.") for believing in me. He embodies what Mother Teresa called "the joy of giving." Finally, I wish to thank Thomas Marsan for his generous hospitality and deep understanding of me as a mystic, poet and pilgrim. Bravo Tom!

This book is not a scholarly work but a careful compilation of recipes from a healthy and creative standpoint. The proceeds from this book, if any, will go to Mother Teresa's *Missionaries of Charity* for "the poorest of the poor."

I have happy memories of being a work-study student at the *Schlesinger Library* of Harvard University in the late 1980's when I was a graduate student of Harvard Divinity School. Therefore, I offer a copy of this book to the *Schlesinger Library* of Harvard University with my cordial regards.

"Now you belong to Heaven and the stars spell out your name" is an excerpt from "Candle in the Wind" sung by Elton John at the funeral of Princess Diana in 1997. The words were composed by Bernie Taupin. Princess Diana knew and revered Mother Teresa and died a few weeks before Mother Teresa's demise.

ACKNOWLEDGEMENTS continued

Grateful thanks to everyone where I am currently employed but due to limited space, every name cannot be written. However, I wish to specifically thank the following people who have been particularly helpful to me. I know that Mother Teresa would have been very appreciative of their kindness towards many people and she would have been delighted that they have included me in their circle of caring and compassion and done so with civility and sensitivity towards me as a fellow human being.

Grateful thanks to Doris Nelson for her moral support and understanding of me both as an employee and as an independent scholar and writer. I commend her ability to help many people with efficiency and good will to all. Grateful thanks to Colby James Peck for his exemplary patience, courtesy, calm efficiency and helpfulness to everyone. I commend his courage, compassion and deep sense of responsibility. (You have a wise head on young shoulders, friend Colby, may God bless you always!).

Grateful thanks to John Vissa for his genuine friendship and kindness over the years. Finally, my grateful thanks to Catherine Lortie, Laura Easton, Benjamin Kelly and Michael Sullivan for their friendship and kindness. Bravo my friends! Dear friends all, I, in turn, remain your loyal and loving friend and co-worker. As Charles Dickens' Tiny Tim would say: "God bless us everyone."

NOTES ON THE PHOTOGRAPHS ON THE FRONT AND BACK COVERS

Pictures on the cover page from left to right :--
potato curry (p.28), rice (p.18), chick peas (p.9), lentils with rice (p.19).
On the left down :--
shrimp and rice (p.31), okra curry (p.29), chicken and yogurt (p.42).
On the right down :--
potatoes and cauliflower (p.39), cucumber and mint salad (p.4), yogurt dips (p.3).

Pictures on the back cover.
First row from left to right:--
fragrant rice (p.12), yogurt dips (p.3), seasoned yellow lentils (p.20).
Second row from left to right:--
cauliflower with peppers (p.27), lamb or turkey curry with rice (p.52), chicken with spicy sauce (p.46).
Third row from left to right :--
shrimp with mango sauce (p.33), chick pea salad (p.8), rice pudding (p.54).

Dear Shuma

The fruit of SILENCE is Prayer
The fruit of PRAYER is Faith
The fruit of FAITH is Love
The fruit of LOVE is Service
The Fruit of SERVICE is Peace

Mother Teresa

God bless you
Lee Teresa mc

I wish to dedicate this book to my very generous and hospitable parents Uma Devi and Judhajit Kumar Chakravarty

and to
Mother Teresa (1910 -1997)
who often asked me " to do small things
with great love " and to do
"something beautiful for God."

"Now you belong to Heaven
And the stars spell out your name."

In 1975, then Prime Minister of India, Indira Gandhi wrote an insightful description of Mother Teresa.

The following is an excerpt from that article by Indira Gandhi about Mother Teresa :

"Who else in this wide world reaches out to the friendless and the needy so naturally, so simply, so effectively?
Tagore wrote ' there rest Thy feet where live the poorest, the lowliest, and lost.' That is where Mother Teresa is to be found-- with no thought of, or slightest discrimination between colour or creed, language or country.
She lives the truth that prayer is devotion, prayer is service. Service is her concern, her religion, her redemption.
To meet her is to feel utterly humble, to sense the power of tenderness, the strength of love."

INTRODUCTION

I have adapted Indian recipes for the American kitchen and I have only included recipes that fit the requirements of "healthy" food. Most people in India are vegetarians. Those who are not, would eat Indian dishes in the following sequence: appetizers, flat bread or rice, lentils, vegetables, fish, poultry, meat, dessert. Such a series of delicacies would be served on very special occasions. Usually a simple meal would consist of flat bread or rice, with a lentil and vegetable dish, an appetizer or relish (called raita or chutney). Dessert in India is often a slice of mango or papaya or a small bowl of sweet yogurt. Obviously the 55 recipes in this book only cover a small segment of India's huge and varied cuisine.

It is my sincere hope that this book will be a healthy, practical and creative resource for cooks.

Shuma Chakravarty
Cohasset, MA.
March, 2013.

Author's note.

Shuma Chakravarty was born in Kolkata, India but has spent most of her life in the United States. She was very fortunate to have known Mother Teresa for many years and to have been greatly loved by her. She is a scholar and a published author of several books. Her poetry and prose have been included in several anthologies. She has graduate degrees in English literature (from Simmons College) and in Theology from Boston University and Harvard University.

Table of Contents

Salad and Relishes..1 - 9

Bread..10

Rice..11-18

Lentils and Home-Made Cheese..19-22

Vegetables..23-30

Seafood and Fish..31-40

Poultry..41-48

Meats..49-53

Desserts..54-55

SALAD AND RELISHES

Salads and Relishes

Mango and Coconut Relish/Chutney

1 large ripe mango
2 tablespoons chopped fresh cilantro leaves
2 fresh green chilies, seeded and chopped

1 tablespoon shredded coconut
1 teaspoon sugar
salt to taste
1 cup golden raisins

Method:

Peel the mango and discard the pit. Place the mango, cilantro, chilies, coconut, sugar and salt in a food processor. Process for 1 minute until smooth. Pour in about 2/3 to 1 ¼ cups of water to achieve a thick paste. Transfer to a serving plate and mix in the raisins.

Serves:	4	Saturated fat:	2 g
Preparation time:	20 min.	Protein:	1 g
Cooking time:	15 min.	Carb:	7 g
Calories per serving:	52	Cholesterol per serving:	N/A
Total fat grams	3 g		

Salads and Relishes

Coconut and Cilantro Relish/Chutney

1 ½ cups shredded coconut
1 green chili, seeded and sliced
2 tablespoons chopped fresh mint

4 tablespoons fresh cilantro leaves
salt to taste

Method:

Place the coconut in a food processor and add the fresh green chili, mint, cilantro and salt. Process for 2 minutes. Remove from the food processor and place in a small serving bowl. Garnish with a sprig of mint. Use within 2 days.

Serves:	4	Saturated fat:	17g
Preparation time:	15 min.	Protein:	2 g
Cooking time:	15 min.	Carb:	2 g
Calories per serving:	191	Cholesterol per serving:	N/A
Total fat grams	19g		

Salads and Relishes

Tomato and Onion Raita with Cucumber
(Raita is a yogurt based dip)

1 ¼ cups low-fat, plain yogurt
1 onion, diced
2 tomatoes, diced
2 fresh green chilies, seeded and chopped (optional)
1 tablespoon chopped fresh cilantro leaves

½ teaspoon sugar
Salt to taste
1 sliced cucumber
Pinch of ground coriander
1 teaspoon of ground cumin
Garnish with a sprig of fresh mint

Method:

In a medium bowl, combine the yogurt, onion, tomatoes, green chilies, cilantro cucumbers, sugar, salt, coriander and cumin. Stir well. Garnish with a sprig of fresh mint serve cold.

Serves:	4	Saturated fat:	1g
Preparation time:	10 min.	Protein:	5g
Cooking time	n/a	Carb:	9g
Calories per serving:	57	Cholesterol per serving:	3mg
Total fat grams	2g		

Salads and Relishes

Cucumber and Mint Raita

½ cucumber
1 ¼ cups low-fat plain yogurt
salt to taste
1 teaspoon sugar
1 fresh green chili, seeded and sliced (optional)

1 teaspoon ground cumin
1 tablespoon chopped, fresh cilantro leaves
fresh mint sprigs for garnish

Method:

Peel and slice the cucumber. In a medium bowl, whisk the yogurt. Add salt, sugar, cumin, chili and cilantro. Add the cucumber and put the mixture in a serving bowl. Stir well. Garnish with mint sprigs and serve.

Serves:	4	Saturated fat:	none
Preparation time:	10 min.	Protein:	4 g
Cooking time:	n/a	Carb:	8g
Calories per serving:	53	Cholesterol per serving:	3 mg
Total fat grams	1g		

Salads and Relishes

Mint and Mango Raita

1 ¼ cups low-fat plain yogurt
1 ripe mango
1 teaspoon mint sauce
½ cucumber sliced
1 tablespoon honey

2 tablespoons chopped, fresh cilantro leaves
salt to taste
½ teaspoon ground cumin powder
fresh mint leaves for garnish

Method:

Whisk the yogurt and place in a serving bowl. Peel the mango, remove the pit, slice the fruit and place it in a food processor. Add the mint sauce, cucumber, honey, cilantro and salt. Process for 1 ½ minutes. Add the mango mixture to the yogurt and stir well. Garnish with mint leaves. Serve cold.

Serves:	4	Saturated fat:	1g
Preparation time:	20 min.	Protein:	5g
Cooking time:	n/a	Carb:	15g
Calories per serving:	82	Cholesterol per serving:	3mg
Total fat grams	1g		

Salads and Relishes

Tomato and Onion Salad

1 red onion, diced
2 tomatoes, diced
1 large carrot, diced
1 medium cucumber, diced
1 fresh green chili, seeded and sliced

1 tablespoon chopped, fresh cilantro leaves
1 tablespoon chopped, fresh mint, plus extra leaves (for garnish)
salt to taste
2 tablespoons lime juice

Method:

Put the diced onion, tomatoes, carrots and cucumber in a salad bowl. Add the chili, herbs and salt to taste. Using a fork, mix everything together. Sprinkle with lime juice and garnish with sprigs of mint.

Serves:	4	Saturated fat:	none
Preparation time:	15 min.	Protein:	1g
Cooking time:	n/a	Carb:	8g
Calories per serving:	39	Cholesterol per serving:	none
Total fat grams	1g		

Salads and Relishes

Spinach and Potato Salad

medium sized sweet potato or Yukon gold potato
1 large carrot sliced
salt to taste

25 small spinach leaves
1 red bell pepper, seeded and sliced
½ green bell pepper, seeded and diced
2 scallions, sliced at an angle

Dressing:

2 tablespoons pine nuts
2 tablespoons golden raisins
5 walnuts
2 tablespoon chopped fresh cilantro leaves

1 teaspoon mild curry powder
1 tablespoon lemon juice
1 tablespoon honey
2 tablespoons low-fat plain yogurt
salt to taste
coarsely ground black pepper

Method:

Slice the potato and cook with the carrot slices in boiling water. On a serving plate toss the spinach leaves, potato and carrot slices. Garnish with the red and green bell peppers and chopped scallions.

To make the dressing, mix in a small bowl the pine nuts, raisins and walnuts. In another bowl, mix the cilantro, curry powder, honey, yogurt and salt to taste. Pour this over the nuts and raisins and blend everything well. Season with coarsely ground black pepper,. Serve the dressing with the salad.

Serves:	4	Saturated fat:	1g
Preparation time:	20 min.	Protein:	17g
Cooking time:	25 min.	Carb:	28g
Calories per serving:	410	Cholesterol per serving:	4mg
Total fat grams	26g	mg.	

Salads and Relishes

Chickpea Salad

1 ½ cups canned chickpeas
1 teaspoon cumin seeds
1 teaspoon coriander seeds
½ red bell pepper, seeded and sliced
½ orange bell pepper, seeded and sliced

½ green bell pepper, seeded and sliced
¼ small red cabbage, shredded
1 iceberg lettuce, shredded
1 large carrot, diced
½ cucumber, sliced
½ red onion, sliced

Dressing:

2 garlic cloves, crushed
salt to taste
1 tablespoon olive oil

2 tablespoons lemon juice
1 pinch of sugar
fresh green chili, seeded and sliced
mint sprigs for garnish

Method:

Drain the chick peas. Toast the cumin and coriander seeds in a non-stick pan for 1 minute. Then grind the seeds. Combine all the ingredients for the salad dressing and stir well. Mix the remaining salad ingredients in a salad bowl. Pour the dressing over the salad and toss the salad. Sprinkle the salad with cumin and coriander seeds. Garnish with mint sprigs.

Serves:	4	Saturated fat:	1g
Preparation time:	20 min.	Protein:	10g
Cooking time:	3 min.	Carb:	24g
Calories per serving:	187	Cholesterol per serving:	none
Total fat grams	7g		

Salads and Relishes
Spicy Chick Peas

4 cups canned chickpeas
1 large potato, cubed
1 medium onion, diced
2 tablespoons tamarind paste (or 3 tablespoons lemon juice)
2 teaspoons mango pulp
1 teaspoon garam masala
1 teaspoon ground coriander
½ teaspoon ground ginger
1 teaspoon curry powder
2 tablespoons ketchup

2 tablespoons sugar
salt to taste
1 tablespoon chopped fresh mint
2 tablespoons chopped fresh cilantro
4 cherry tomatoes, sliced
3 small onions, sliced
2 green chilies seeded and sliced for garnish
2 teaspoons shredded coconut
1 sliced cucumber

Method:

Drain the chickpeas and place them in a large serving. Bowl. In a large bowl, blend together the tamarind paste, mango pulp, garam masala, ground coriander, ginger, curry powder, ketchup, sugar, salt and 2/3 cup water. Pour this sauce over the chickpeas. Add the potato and onion and mix well. Mix in half of the mint and cilantro. Garnish with the remaining mint and cilantro, tomatoes and onions. Garnish with the seeded green chilies and shredded coconut. Serve cold with sliced cucumbers and pita bread.

Serves:	4	Saturated fat:	1g
Preparation time:	20 min.	Protein:	1 g
Cooking time:	10 min.	Carb:	61g
Calories per serving:	354	Cholesterol per serving:	none
Total fat grams	6g		

BREAD

Bread

NAAN
(Yeasted Bread)

1 teaspoon sugar
1 teaspoon compressed fresh yeast
2/3 cup warm water
2 cups all purpose flour, more for dusting the Naan

1 tablespoon melted butter
1 teaspoon salt
1/4 cup olive oil
1 teaspoon sesame seeds or poppy seeds
corn oil for brushing the grill pan

Method:

Put the sugar and yeast in a cup with the warm water. Mix well until the yeast has dissolved and leave for 10 minutes until frothy. Place the flour in a large mixing bowl. Make a well in the middle, add the butter and salt and pour in the yeast mixture. Mix well, using your hands and adding a little more water if needed to achieve a soft and pliable dough. Turn the dough out onto a floured surface and knead for 5 minutes until smooth. Place the dough back in the bowl, cover and leave to rise in a warm place for 3 to 4 hours, until doubled in size, Preheat the broiler and line the broiler pan with foil. Grease the foil with corn oil.

Turn the dough out on a floured surface and knead it for an additional 2 minutes. Break it into 6 balls with your hand and pat these rounds about 5 inches in diameter and ½ thick.

Place 2 or 3 rounds in the broiler pan, brush with olive oil and sprinkle with sesame or poppy seeds. Broil for 7 to 10 minutes, turning twice, brushing with oil and sprinkling with seeds and each time, until golden and lightly puffed. Wrap bread in foil to keep warm while you cook the rest. Serve warm as soon as all are cooked.

Serves:	6	**Saturated fat:**	11g
Preparation time: plus 3-4 hours rising	25 min	**Protein:**	6g
		Carb:	50g
Cooking time:	15-20 min	**Cholesterol:**	11mg
Calories per serving:	350		
Total fat grams:	19g		

RICE

Spicy Rice with Stir-Fried Vegetables

2 cups Basmati rice
2 tablespoons corn oil
6 bay leaves
½ teaspoon mixed mustard and cumin seeds
1 teaspoon garlic pulp
1 teaspoon ginger pulp
1 onion chopped
2 tomatoes, sliced
2 oz. Corn kernels
2 oz. shelled (or frozen) peas
1 oz. green beans, cut into pieces
1 carrot, diced
2 tablespoons lemon juice
2 tablespoons chopped fresh cilantro leaves
2 fresh green chilies, seeded and sliced (for garnish)
Parsley leaves (for garnish)
Salt to taste

Method:

Wash the rice until the water runs clear and soak it in water. Heat the oil in a large, heavy-bottomed saucepan over moderate heat. Add the bay leaves and mixed seeds and fry for 3 minutes. Add the vegetables beginning with the tomatoes and stir-fry for 2 minutes. Add the lemon juice, cilantro and salt to taste. Drain the rice, add rice to the vegetables and stir-fry for 1 minute. Add 4 cups of water and bring to a boil. Reduce the heat to medium and cover the dish. Cook for 15-20 minutes until all the water is absorbed and the rice is cooked. Remove from heat. Let stand covered for 5 minutes before serving. Garnish with sliced green chilies (optional) and parsley.

Serves:	4	Saturated fat:	1g
Preparation time:	20 min.	Protein:	8g
Cooking time:	30-35 min.	Carb:	61g
Calories per serving:	338	Cholesterol per serving:	none
Total fat grams	7g		

Rice

Fragrant Rice with Raisins

2 cups Basmati rice
2 cardamom pods
¼ teaspoon black cumin seeds
1 cinnamon stick
4 black peppercorns

2 bay leaves
salt to taste
3 oz. Peas
½ cup golden raisins (for garnish)
fried onion slices (optional - for garnish)

Method:

Wash the rice until the water runs clear and soak it in water. Pour 3 cups of water into a large saucepan, add the whole spices and the salt. Place the saucepan over high heat and lower the heat when the water begins to boil. Drain the rice and add it to the water with the peas. Cover with a lid and cook over medium heat for 15 minutes until all the water is absorbed and the rice is cooked. Remove the rice from the heat. Let it stand for 5 minutes in a covered pan. Garnish with the golden raisins and fried onions. Serve with a slotted spoon.

Serves:	4	**Saturated Fat:**	None
Preparation time	5 min.	**Protein:**	6 g
Cooking time:	15-20 min.	**Carb:**	52 g
plus 5 min. standing		**Cholesterol per serving:**	None
Calories per serving:	238		
Total fat grams	1 g		

Rice

Rice with Nuts and Fruit

4 tablespoons corn oil
1 large onion, chopped
2 garlic cloves, crushed
1 inch piece fresh ginger root, finely chopped
1 teaspoon coriander
1 teaspoon cumin
1 tablespoon mild curry powder
1 ½ cups Basmati rice

3 ½ cups boiling fat-free vegetable broth
14 oz. can chopped tomatoes
¾ cup dried apricots, cut into slivers
1 red bell pepper, seeded and diced
¾ peas
1 small banana
½ toasted mixed nuts

Method:

Heat the oil in a large saucepan. Add the onion and stir-fry for 3 minutes. Stir in the garlic, ginger, coriander, cumin, curry powder and rice. Mix everything and stir constantly for 2 minutes. Pour in the boiling vegetable broth and add the tomatoes, salt and pepper. Bring the mixture to a boil, reduce the heat, cover the pan and cook for 40 minutes or until the liquid is almost absorbed. Add the apricots, red bell pepper and peas to the rice mixture. Cover and continue cooking for 10 minutes. Remove the pan from the heat and leave dish covered for 5 minutes. Peel and slice the banana. Add the toasted nuts and sliced banana to the rice mixture and toss lightly. Transfer the rice, fruit and nut mixture to a serving dish. Serve hot.

Serves:	4-6	Saturated fat:	4g
Preparation time:	20 min.	Protein:	6g
Cooking time:	24-30 min.	Carb:	56g
Calories per serving:	322	Cholesterol per serving:	None
Total fat grams	8g		

Rice with Peas

2 cups Basmati rice
1 tablespoon olive oil
1 tablespoon corn oil
1 medium onion, sliced
1 teaspoon ginger pulp
1 teaspoon garlic pulp
salt to taste
1 bay leaf

3 whole cloves
1 small piece cinnamon stick
8 black peppercorns
2 whole black cardamom pods
3 oz. shelled peas (or frozen peas)
Some whole cilantro leaves for garnish.

Method:

Wash the rice and let soak it in water. Heat the oils in a heavy-bottomed saucepan. Add the onion and fry over moderate heat until golden. Add the ginger, garlic, salt to taste, bay leaf, cloves, cinnamon, peppercorns and cardamom. Cook for about 30 seconds. Drain the rice and add to the oil. Stir gently. Add the peas. Pour in 3 cups of water and bring to a boil. Lower the heat, cover the pan and cook for 15 minutes until the water is absorbed and the rice is cooked. Once the rice is cooked, remove from the heat and keep it covered for 5 minutes. Serve hot and garnish with fresh cilantro leaves.

Serves:	4	Saturated fat:	1 g
Preparation time:	10 min.	Protein:	6 g
Cooking time:	20-25 min.	Carb:	52
Plus 5 min. standing			
Total fat grams:	5g	Cholesterol per serving:	None

Rice with Tomatoes

2 cups Basmati rice
2 tablespoons corn oil
1 medium onion, sliced
1 teaspoon onion powder
8 bay leaves

½ teaspoon ginger pulp
½ teaspoon garlic pulp
2 tomatoes, sliced
salt to taste
2 oz. shelled peas

Method:

Wash the rice until the water runs clear. Leave it to soak in fresh water. Heat the oil in a large, heavy-bottomed saucepan over moderate heat. Add the onion, onion powder and bay leaves and fry for 5 minutes. Add the ginger, garlic, tomato and salt. Stir-fry for 3 minutes. Drain the rice and add to the pan stirring gently for 1 minute. Add the peas and 4 cups of water. Bring to a boil. Lower the heat, cover the pan and cook over low heat for 15 to 20 minutes until all of the water is absorbed and the rice is tender.

Serves:	4	Saturated fat:	1g
Preparation time:	10 min.	Protein:	6g
Cooking time:	30-35 min.	Carb:	56g
Calories per serving:	282	Cholesterol per serving:	None
Total fat grams	4g		

Rice

Rice with Shredded Coconut

2 cups Basmati rice
2 tablespoons corn oil
6 bay leaves
1 tablespoon onion powder
1 medium onion, sliced

2 garlic cloves
1 teaspoon shredded ginger
Salt to taste
1 large carrot, diced
2 tablespoon shredded coconut
1 tablespoon chopped, fresh cilantro leaves

Method:

Wash the Basmati rice until the water runs clear. Let the rice soak in water. Heat the oil in a heavy-bottomed saucepan over moderate heat. Add the bay leaves, onion slices, onion powder and stir-fry for 2 minutes. Add the garlic, ginger, salt, carrots, 1 tablespoon shredded coconut and ½ tablespoon of cilantro leaves. Mix well.

Drain the rice and add it to the onion mixture. Stir-fry for 1 minute. Add the remaining coconut, cilantro and 4 cups of water Bring to a boil, lower the heat to moderate. Cover and cook for 20 minutes, until the rice is tender. Let the rice stand off the heat for 5 minutes before serving. Garnish with a sprinkle of shredded coconut.

Serves:	4	Saturated fat:	4g
Preparation time:	20 min.	Protein:	6g
Plus 5 min. standing		Carb:	56g
Calories per serving :	322		
Total fat grams:	8g	Cholesterol per serving: None	

Rice with Vegetables and Beans

2 cups Basmati rice
5 oz. canned red kidney beans
2 tablespoons corn oil
1 cinnamon stick
1 bay leaf
2 cloves
3 green cardamom pods
4 black peppercorns
1 onion sliced
1 teaspoon ginger pulp
1 teaspoon garlic pulp
1 teaspoon mild curry powder
½ teaspoon turmeric
1 teaspoon garam masala
1 teaspoon ground coriander seeds
2 oz. shelled peas
2 oz. cauliflower florets
1 large carrot sliced
2 tablespoons low-fat plain yogurt
salt to taste
2 tablespoons chopped fresh cilantro leaves
1 red bell pepper, seeded and diced
1 tablespoon lemon juice

Method:

Wash the rice until the water runs clear and soak the rice in water. Drain the liquid from the kidney beans and set aside. In a large, heavy-bottomed saucepan, heat the corn oil over moderate heat. Add the cinnamon stick, bay leaf, cloves, cardamom pods and peppercorns and cook for 1 minute. Add the onions and fry for 2 minutes. Lower the heat and add the ginger, garlic, curry powder, turmeric, garam masala and ground coriander, followed by all the vegetables. Stir-fry for 2 minutes and then stir in the yogurt.

Drain the rice and add it and the beans to the pan. Using a slotted spoon stir the mixture without breaking up the rice. Add salt to taste, half the cilantro, red bell pepper slices, lemon juice and 3 cups of water. Bring to a boil, then turn down the heat to moderate. Cover the pan with a lid and cook for 15 minutes until the water has been absorbed and the rice is cooked. Remove from heat. Let the dish stand for 5 minutes. Garnish with the remaining cilantro leaves.

Serves:	4	Saturated fat:	4g
Preparation time:	25 min.	Protein:	10g
Cooking time:	25 min	Carb:	58g
Plus 5 min. standing		Cholesterol per serving:	None
Calories per serving	331		
Total fat grams	7g		

Rice

Rice with Mustard Seeds

2 cups Basmati rice
1 tablespoon corn oil
¼ teaspoon mustard seeds
4 bay leaves
½ teaspoon ginger pulp

½ teaspoon garlic pulp
salt to taste
2 tablespoons pine nuts
some whole cilantro leaves (for garnish)

Method:

Wash the rice until the water runs clear. Leave it to soak in water. Heat the oil in a large, heavy-bottomed saucepan. Add the mustard seeds and bay leaves and fry for 30 seconds. Drain the water from the rice and pour the rice into the pan. Continue its stir-fry for 30 seconds. Pour in 4 cups of water. Bring to a boil, then reduce the heat to moderate. Cover the pan and cook for 15-20 minutes until all the water is absorbed and the rice is cooked. Let the rice stand off the heat for 5 minutes. Serve hot with a few cilantro leaves for garnish.

Serves:	4	Saturated Fat:	1g
Preparation time:	10 min.	Protein:	6g
Cooking time:	20-25 min.	Carb:	51g
plus 5 min. standing		Cholesterol per serving:	None
Calories per serving:	306		
Total fat grams	9g		

Lentils and Rice with Vegetables

2 cups Basmati rice
1 cup masoor dhal (red or pink lentils)
2 tablespoons corn oil
6 bay leaves
1 medium onion sliced
1 teaspoon mild curry powder
1 teaspoon garlic pulp
1 teaspoon ginger pulp
½ teaspoon turmeric powder
1 medium size carrot, diced
1 oz. shelled peas
2 oz. green beans, sliced into small pieces
salt to taste
1 tablespoon chopped fresh cilantro leaves plus whole leaves for garnish

Method:

Wash the rice and lentils and soak in a bowl of water. Heat the oil in a wok or deep pan. Add the bay leaves, curry powder and onion slices and fry for 2 minutes. Lower the heat and add the ginger, garlic, turmeric, carrot, peas, green beans and salt.

Drain the water from the rice and lentils and add to the spiced mixture. Stir everything for 2 minutes, then add 4 cups of water. Stir again and add the chopped cilantro. When the water begins to boil, lower the heat, cover the pan and cook for 15-20 minutes until the rice and lentils are thoroughly cooked and the water has evaporated. Leave the dish to stand for 5 minutes, after removing from heat. Garnish with whole cilantro leaves.

Serves:	4-6	Saturated Fat:	1g
Preparation time	20 min	Protein:	15g
Cooking time:	25-30 min.	Carb:	72g
plus 5 min. standing		Cholesterol per serving:	None
Calories per serving:	407		
Total fat grams	7g		

Seasoned Yellow Split Peas

1 cup moong dahl (or yellow split peas)
1 ½ tablespoons corn oil
1 teaspoon mixed fennel seeds, crushed coriander seeds and cumin seeds
1 medium size onion, sliced
1 teaspoon ginger pulp

1 teaspoon garlic pulp
1 teaspoon mild curry powder
salt to taste
2 fresh green chilies, sliced and seeded (optional)
1 red bell pepper, seeded and sliced
1 tablespoon fresh cilantro leaves for garnish

Method:
Wash the yellow split peas/moong dhal and cover with 2 cups of water in a heavy bottomed pan. Cook for 15 to 20 minutes over moderate heat, stirring occasionally until the split peas are cooked. Drain the water. Heat the oil in a large pan. Add the mixed seeds and fry for 30 seconds over moderate heat. Add the onion and stir-fry for 3 minutes until softened. Add the ginger, garlic, curry powder and salt to taste. Add the boiled split peas and stir everything with a wooden spoon. Pour in 2/3 cup of water and add the chilies if desired. Lower the heat, cover the pan and cook for 5 minutes. Serve this dish garnished with fresh cilantro leaves and slices of red bell pepper.

Serves:	4	Saturated fat:	1g
Preparation time:	20 min.	Protein:	10g
Cooking time:	35 min.	Carb:	28g
Calories per serving:	193	Cholesterol per serving:	None
Total fat grams	6g		

Chana Dhal with Home Made Cheese and Tomatoes

6 oz. Chana dhal (a variety of chick peas) or yellow split peas
1 onion diced
1 teaspoon garam masala
1 teaspoon garlic pulp
1 teaspoon ginger pulp
½ teaspoon chili powder (optional)
2 teaspoons mango pulp
salt to taste
chopped fresh cilantro leaves for garnish

Seasoned Oil

1 tablespoon corn oil
½ teaspoon white cumin seeds
4 bay leaves
3 whole garlic cloves
6 small onions, peeled
6 bite sized cubes of home-made cheese/panir (recipe follows)
6 cherry tomatoes

Method:
Wash the chana dhal or split peas. Place in a large saucepan with the onion, garam masala, garlic, ginger, chili powder, mango pulp, salt and 2 ½ cups of water. Bring to a boil and cook for 15 minutes over medium heat, stirring occasionally.
To prepare the seasoned oil, heat the oil over moderate heat. Add the cumin seeds, bay leaves, garlic cloves, onions, cheese cubes, cherry tomatoes and stir-fry for 2 minutes. Once the split peas are cooked and the water is absorbed, pour the seasoned oil over the split peas and mix well. Garnish with chopped cilantro. Serve with boiled basmati rice.

Serves:	4	Saturated fat:	2g
Preparation time:	15 min.	Protein:	15g
Cooking time:	20 min.	Carb:	41g
Calories per serving:	274	Cholesterol per serving:	15 mg
Total fat grams	7g		

Panir or Home-Made Cheese

4 ½ cups low-fat milk
1 tablespoons of fresh lemon juice

Method:

Slowly boil the milk over low heat. Add the lemon juice to the boiling milk, stirring constantly until the milk thickens and begins to curdle. Strain the curdled milk through a sieve. Set aside the strained curds between 2 chopping boards and put a heavy weight on top for 2 hours to strain the water and to press the curds to a flat shape, ½ inch thick. Then the panir can be cut like cheese.

Serves:	4	Saturated Fat:	3g
Preparation time:	10 min.	Protein:	8g
plus 1 ½ -2 hrs. setting		Carb:	13g
Cooking time:	20 min.	Cholesterol per serving:	18g
Calories per serving:	116		
Total fat grams:	4g		

VEGETABLES

Vegetables

Zucchini and Eggplant in a Mint Yogurt Sauce

1 medium eggplant
1 ¼ cups low-fat plain yogurt
1 teaspoon mint sauce
1 tablespoon fresh, chopped mint
1 teaspoon sugar
salt to taste
1 tablespoon corn oil

6 bay leaves
¼ teaspoon white cumin seeds
1 large zucchini, sliced
1 tablespoon chopped, fresh cilantro leaves (for garnish)
1 red bell pepper, seeded and sliced (for garnish)

Method:

Preheat the oven to 375 degrees F. Cut off the top of the eggplant and bake it in the oven for 20-25 minutes. When the baked eggplant is cooled, remove its skin and mash the eggplant. In a large bowl, whisk the yogurt and mix it with the mashed eggplant, mint sauce, fresh mint, sugar and salt. Set aside.

Heat the oil in a wok or deep frying pan. Add the bay leaves, white cumin seeds and zucchini slices and stir-fry for 1 ½ minutes over moderate heat. Pour the zucchini and seasoned oil over the yogurt and eggplant. Mix well. Garnish with cilantro leaves and red bell pepper slices. Serve hot.

Serves:	4	Saturated fat:	1g
Preparation time:	25 min.	**Protein:**	5g
Cooking time:	25-30 min.	**Carb:**	9g
Calories per serving:	85	**Cholesterol per serving:**	3mg
Total fat grams:	4g		

Vegetables

Potato and Eggs with Indian Sauce

4 large hard boiled eggs
2 tablespoons tomato puree
1 tablespoon ground coriander
1 teaspoon ground cardamom
2 large potatoes, boiled and sliced thickly
1 teaspoon ginger pulp
1 teaspoon garlic pulp
1 tablespoon shredded coconut
2 tablespoons coconut milk
1 teaspoon curry powder
2 tablespoons sunflower oil
1 green bell pepper, seeded and sliced
2 tablespoons chopped, fresh cilantro
Fresh basil leaves and tomato wedges for garnish

Method:

Shell the eggs and cut them in half lengthwise. Arrange the egg halves on a serving platter. Make a paste in a bowl by combining the tomato puree, ground coriander, cardamom, ginger, garlic, shredded coconut and curry powder. Blend together and stir in 1 ½ cups water. Heat the oil in a wok or deep frying pan over moderate heat. Pour in the spice mixture, lower the heat and cook for 5 minutes over low heat, stirring occasionally. Add the green bell pepper slices and cilantro. Cook for 2 minutes. Stir well. Remove from heat. Pour the sauce over the eggs and garnish with fresh basil leaves and tomato wedges.

Serves:	4	Saturated fat:	6 g
Preparation time:	15 min.	Protein:	8 g
Cooking time:	10-12 min.	Carb:	25 g
Calories per serving:	224	Cholesterol per serving:	193 mg
Total fat grams	17g		

Vegetables

Eggplant with Onions and Tomatoes

1 large eggplant
2 onions
2 tablespoons corn oil
1 teaspoon mustard seeds
4 bay leaves
1 tablespoon tomato puree
1 tablespoon ground coriander
2 tomatoes, seeded and diced

1 fresh green chili, seeded and sliced for garnish
1 tablespoon chopped, fresh cilantro leaves
1 tablespoon lemon juice
salt to taste
1 teaspoon garlic pulp
1 teaspoon ginger pulp\
1 sliced and seeded red bell pepper for garnish

Method:

Wash the eggplant and cut into very small pieces and place in a bowl. Chop the onions finely. Heat the oil in a medium saucepan over moderate heat and add the mustard seeds, bay leaves and onions. Lower the heat and add the tomato puree, ground coriander, garlic, ginger, salt and lemon juice stirring constantly. Cook for 5 minutes, stirring often, until the onions are softened.
Add the eggplant and stir-fry for 2 minutes. Stir in 2/3 cup water, cover the pan and cook over low heat for 7 minutes, stirring occasionally. Add the fresh cilantro and tomatoes. Stir for 1 minute. Remove from heat. Garnish with red bell pepper strips. Serve hot.

Serves:	4	Saturated fat:	1g
Preparation time:	20 min.	Protein:	3g
Cooking time:	15 min.	Carb:	11g
Calories per serving:	105	Cholesterol per serving:	None
Total fat grams	6g		

Vegetables

Peas with Panir (Home-Made Cheese)

1 large carrot, chopped
1 red bell pepper, seeded and sliced
1 ½ tablespoons corn oil
2 medium onions, finely chopped
8 oz. corn kernels
4 ½ oz. Peas
1 inch piece ginger, grated

2 garlic cloves, finely chopped
1 ½ teaspoons mild curry powder
salt to taste
12 cubes of panir
sprigs of fresh cilantro leaves (for garnish)
sprigs of fresh mint leaves (for garnish)

Method:

Heat the oil over moderate heat. Add the chopped onions and fry for 3 minutes. Stir well. Add the corn, peas, carrot, bell pepper, ginger, garlic, curry powder and salt. Continue to stir-fry over moderate heat for 5 minutes. Garnish with mint and cilantro. Serve hot.

Serves:	4	Saturated fat:	1g
Preparation time:	10 min.	Protein:	5g
Cooking time:	12-15 min.	Carb:	23g
Calories per serving:	145	Cholesterol per serving:	None
Total fat grams	5g		

Vegetables

Cauliflower with Peppers

2 small cauliflowers or 1 medium size cauliflower, cut into small florets
8 small potatoes, sliced
1 red bell pepper
1 green bell pepper
1 yellow bell pepper
2 oz. Peas
1 tablespoon corn oil
¼ teaspoon white cumin seeds
6 bay leaves
2 teaspoons curry powder
2 onions sliced
3 garlic cloves, chopped
2 teaspoons shredded ginger
½ teaspoon turmeric
salt to taste
1 tablespoon chopped fresh cilantro leaves for garnish

Method:

Pour the oil into a heavy-bottomed sauce pan over moderate heat and stir-fry the bay leaves and cumin seeds for 1 minute. Add the garlic, onions and ginger and cook for 2 minutes, constantly stirring the mixture. Add all the vegetables, the curry powder and salt. Mix all ingredients together. Add 1cup of water and cook for 7 minutes over low heat, covered with a lid. Remove from heat and garnish with cilantro leaves. Serve hot.

Serves:	4	Saturated fat:	1g
Preparation time:	20 min.	Protein:	8g
Cooking time:	12-15 min.	Carb:	30g
Calories per serving:	185	Cholesterol per serving:	None
Total fat grams:	4g		

Vegetables

Potato Curry

15 small potatoes

1 tablespoon lemon juice
2 teaspoons curry powder
1 ½ teaspoons ground coriander
1 teaspoon garlic pulp
2 teaspoon ginger pulp
salt to taste
1 ½ tablespoons corn oil
4 bay leaves

3 onions finely chopped

1 green bell pepper, seeded and coarsely chopped
3 oz. peas
2 tablespoons chopped fresh cilantro leaves
2 chopped large tomatoes

Method:

Boil the potatoes, cut potatoes in half. In a bowl mix the lemon juice, curry powder, ground coriander, garlic, ginger and salt. Mix into paste with 1 ½ cups of water. Heat the oil over moderate heat in a heavy bottomed pan. Add the bay leaves, onions, peas and tomatoes and stir-fry for 3 minutes. Take the spice paste from the mixing bowl and pour into the pan. Cook for another 3 minutes. Stir well. Add the potatoes and ½ cup of water. Cover and cook over low heat for 7 minutes. Remove the lid and stir. Add the bell pepper and cilantro and serve hot.

Serves:	4	Saturated fat:	1g
Preparation time:	25 min.	Protein:	13g
Cooking time:	20-25 min.	Carb:	99g
Calories per serving:	469	Cholesterol per serving:	None
Total fat grams	5g		

Vegetables

Okra Curry

1 lb. Okra
10 small potatoes/or new potatoes
Salt to taste
2 tablespoons corn oil
3 onions, sliced
1 tablespoon onion seeds
1 tablespoon fennel seeds
1 tablespoon mustard seeds

1 teaspoon mild curry powder
4 garlic cloves, sliced
2 tomatoes, sliced
2 tablespoons chopped fresh cilantro leaves
1 fresh green chili, seeded and sliced for garnish
1 tablespoon lemon juice
whole cilantro leaves for garnish

Method:
Cut the okra and potatoes in half. Cook the potatoes in boiling water until tender but firm in shape. Drain and set aside.

In a heavy-bottomed sauce pan heat the oil over moderate heat. Fry the onions with the mixed seeds until the onions are golden. Add the curry powder and garlic and stir-fry for 1 minute. Then add the tomatoes, okra, lemon juice and salt. Lower the heat, cover the pan and cook for 5-7 minutes.

Add the potato halves, cover again and cook for 3-5 minutes. Garnish with sliced green chilies and whole cilantro leaves. Serve hot.

Serves:	4	Saturated fat:	1g
Preparation time:	15 min.	Protein:	7g
Cooking time:	25-30 min.	Carb:	33g
Calories per serving:	220	Cholesterol per serving:	None
Total fat grams	7g		

Vegetables

Vegetable Stir-Fry

1 teaspoon canola oil
2 teaspoons mild curry powder
1 teaspoon ground cumin
½ teaspoon parsley flakes
1 ½ teaspoons ground coriander
2 cloves garlic, minced

1 medium onion sliced
1 cup chopped and seeded red bell pepper
1 cup thinly sliced carrots
3 cups cauliflower florets
salt to taste
1 cup water

Method:

Heat oil in large, non-stick skillet over medium heat. Add curry powder, cumin, coriander and parsley flakes, stir-fry for 30 seconds. Stir in the garlic and onion. Add bell pepper, carrots and cauliflower. Reduce heat. Add ½ cup water. Cook and stir until water evaporates. Add remaining ½ cup water, cover and cook for 8 to 10 minutes until the vegetables are tender, stirring occasionally. Add salt and mix well. Sprinkle with cilantro leaves and garnish with red bell pepper slices. Serve hot.

Serves:	6	Saturated fat:	1g
Preparation time:	10 min.	Protein:	6g
Cooking time:	10 min.	Carb:	6g
Calories per serving:	60	Cholesterol per serving:	None
Total fat grams	3g		

SEAFOOD AND FISH

Seafood and Fish

Shrimp with Bell Peppers

6 oz. peeled cooked shrimp
2 tablespoons corn oil
2 onions, diced
1 bay leaf
½ teaspoon cumin powder
2 garlic cloves, sliced in half
1 teaspoon ginger pulp or ginger powder

½ teaspoon chili powder (optional)
½ teaspoon coriander
salt to taste
1 1/2 cups shelled peas
1 green bell pepper, seeded and sliced
1 large red pepper, seeded and coarsely chopped
juice of ½ lemon.

Method:

Rinse the shrimp and dry with a paper towel. In a wok or deep frying pan heat the oil over moderate heat. Add the onions, bay leaf and cumin and fry for 2 minutes. Add the garlic, ginger, chili powder, coriander and salt. Stir fry over low heat for one minute. Add the shrimp and stir fry for 4 minutes. Add the peas, red pepper and cilantro. Cover and cook for 6 minutes, stirring occasionally. Sprinkle with fresh lemon juice and garnish with cilantro leaves.

Serves:	4	Saturated fat:	1g
Preparation time:	15 min.	Protein:	14g
Cooking time:	15-20 min.	Carb:	13g
Calories per serving:	169	Cholesterol per serving:	123mg
Total fat grams :	7g		

Seafood and Fish

Jumbo Shrimp with Mushrooms

8 oz. fresh or frozen jumbo shrimp
2 cups mushrooms
2 tablespoons corn oil
2 medium onions, sliced
½ teaspoon fennel seeds (or 1 teaspoon dried or fresh chopped chives)
2 teaspoons fresh basil leaves, chopped

2 garlic cloves sliced
1 green bell pepper, diced and seeded
2 tablespoons chopped, fresh cilantro leaves
1 stalk of celery, peeled and chopped
2 medium or large chopped fresh tomatoes

Method:

If using fresh shrimp, peel and remove the vein. If using frozen shrimp, defrost and dry with paper towels. Slice the mushrooms into thick pieces. Heat the oil in a wok or deep frying pan. Add the sliced onions, herbs and vegetables for a few minutes. Put the shrimp into the pan and stir occasionally for 8 to 10 minutes. Sprinkle the cilantro leaves on the top for garnish.

Serves:	4	Saturated fat:	1g
Preparation time:	15 min.	Protein:	13g
Cooking time:	10-15 min.	Carb:	8g
Calories per serving:	138	Cholesterol per serving:	110mg
Total fat grams	6g		

Seafood and Fish
Shrimp with Mango

16 peeled, cooked jumbo shrimp
2 tablespoons corn oil
4 onions, thinly sliced
1 tablespoon onion powder
4 bay leaves
1 teaspoon garlic pulp
1 teaspoon ginger pulp
salt to taste

1 teaspoon curry powder
½ teaspoon turmeric
½ cup mango pulp
2 medium tomatoes, quartered
1 tablespoon chopped, fresh cilantro
1 green pepper, seeded and sliced for garnish

Method:

Rinse the shrimp and dry with a paper towel. Heat the oil over moderate heat in a wok or deep frying pan. Add the onions and cook until they are golden brown. Add the bay leaves and onion powder and stir-fry for 2 minutes. Add the garlic, ginger, chili powder, salt, turmeric and mango pulp and stir fry for 3 minutes. Add the shrimp, tomatoes and most of the cilantro leaves. Lower the heat, cover the pan and cook for 7 minutes until the shrimp are firm. Garnish with the remaining cilantro leaves and the green bell pepper slices. Serve hot with cooked Basmati rice.

Serves:	4	Saturated fat:	1g
Preparation time:	15 min.	Protein:	11g
Cooking time:	20-25 min.	Carb:	13g
Calories per serving:	149	Cholesterol per serving:	105mg
Total fat grams	6g		

Seafood and Fish

Golden Fish with Mustard Sauce

1 teaspoon turmeric powder
1 teaspoon salt
2 ½ lbs. Cod fillet, skinned and cut into pieces
6 tablespoons corn oil
4 fresh green chilies, seeded and sliced
1 tablespoon finely chopped, fresh ginger
1 teaspoon crushed garlic
2 medium onions, finely chopped
2 tomatoes, finely chopped
6 tablespoons mustard oil (if you cannot find mustard oil use olive oil but add 2 tablespoons of prepared mustard to flavor the sauce)
2 cups water
Garnish with fresh cilantro leaves

Method:

Mix together the turmeric and salt in a small bowl. Spoon the turmeric and salt mixture over the fish pieces. Heat the oil in a skillet. Add the fish and fry until pale golden yellow. Remove the fish with a slotted spoon and set aside.
Grind the green chilies, ginger, garlic, onions, tomatoes and mustard oil in a food processor to form a paste. Transfer the spice paste into a sauce pan and stir-fry until golden brown. Remove the pan from the heat and gently put the fish pieces into the spice mixture. Place the pan over moderate heat, add water, cook the fish, uncovered for 15-20 minutes until tender. Remove from heat, garnish with cilantro leaves and serve hot with Basmati rice.

Serves:	4	Saturated fat:	1g
Preparation time:	10 min.	Protein:	14g
Cooking time:	10-15 min.	Carb:	7g
Calories per serving:	149	Cholesterol per serving:	27mg
Total fat grams	8g		

Seafood and Fish

Spicy Cod Fillets

4 large, skinless cod fillets
2 tablespoons "gram flour" or "besan (made of ground chick peas). (You can use corn flour mixed with 1 teaspoon of curry powder)
1 tablespoon all purpose flour
1 tablespoon mango powder (you can use orange peel instead)
1 teaspoon mild curry powder
1 teaspoon ground ginger
1 teaspoon garlic powder
salt to taste
2 teaspoons coriander powder
2 tablespoons corn oil
lemon wedges
cucumber slices
red bell pepper strips for garnish

Method:

Rinse the cod fillets and dry with a paper towel and refrigerate. Mix together the flours, mango powder, ginger, garlic powder, salt and coriander powder. Remove the fish from the refrigerator. Dust with the flour and spice mixture. Set aside.

Heat half the oil in a large, nonstick frying pan. Place 2 fish fillets in the oil. Reduce the heat and cook for 2-3 minutes each side, turning the fish until it is thoroughly cooked. Transfer the cooked fillets to a warmed platter and cook the remaining fish in the same way. Decorate with lemon wedges and strips of red bell pepper and cucumber slices. Serve the fish hot with rice.

Serves:	4	Saturated fat:	1g
Preparation time:	15 min.	Protein:	36g
Cooking time:	10 min.	Carb:	9g
Calories per serving:	241	Cholesterol per serving:	78mg
Total fat grams	7g		

Seafood and Fish

Fish with Vegetables

10 oz. fish fillets
2 tablespoons olive oil
1 bay leaf
3 garlic cloves
1 large leek, sliced
6 black peppercorns, crushed
salt to taste
2 tablespoons of lemon juice
1 teaspoon chili powder (optional)

2 carrots, finely chopped
2 potatoes, finely chopped
1 large tomato, chopped
1 tablespoon fresh, chopped mint
1 tablespoon chopped green scallion
1 tablespoon chopped fresh cilantro leaves
fresh mint and cilantro leaves and sliced tomato for garnish

Method:

Cut the fish into cubes. Heat the olive oil over moderate heat in a wok or deep frying pan. Add the bay leaf, garlic, leek, pepper corns and chili powder. Cook for 2-3 minutes and stir well. Add the carrots and potatoes and sprinkle with salt. Cook over low heat for 3 minutes, stirring occasionally. Remove from the heat, add the fish cubes and mix the ingredients well before returning the pan to the heat and stir fry for 6 minutes or until the fish is tender. Add the mint and cilantro leaves and cover and cook on low heat for another 6 minutes. Sprinkle the lemon juice over the fish. Garnish with fresh mint and cilantro leaves.

Serves:	4	Saturated fat:	1g
Preparation time:	20 min.	Protein:	14g
Cooking time:	20-25 min.	Carb:	19g
Calories per serving:	191	Cholesterol per serving:	10mg
Total fat grams	7g		

Seafood and Fish

Fish with Fenugreek or Basil Sauce

4 large skinless sole or flounder fillets
2 tablespoons low-fat sour cream
½ teaspoon turmeric powder
1 teaspoon garlic pulp
1 teaspoon fenugreek
fresh fenugreek or basil leaves
1 teaspoon ground coriander
salt to taste
2 tablespoons olive oil
1 teaspoon mustard seeds
6 bay leaves
1 tablespoon fresh cilantro leaves
8 cherry tomatoes for garnish
1 fresh green chili, seeded, halved lengthwise for garnish

Method:

Wash the fish, dry with a paper towel and place in a greased baking dish. Pour the sour cream into a mixing bowl and add the turmeric, garlic, fennugreek, coriander, salt and 1 ¼ cups of water. Mix well.
Heat the olive oil over medium heat. Add the mustard seeds, bay leaves. Stir fry for 30 seconds, then remove the pan from the heat. Add the sour cream sauce to the pan and mix well. Cook over low heat for 4 minutes. Add the fenugreek or basil leaves and then pour the sauce over the fish. Preheat the oven to 375 degrees F. Place the fish fillets with sauce in the oven and bake for 7 to 10 minutes until the fish is tender. Garnish with cherry tomatoes, basil leaves and green chili strips.

Serves:	4	**Saturated fat:**	2g
Preparation time:	10 min.	**Protein:**	23g
Cooking time:	20 min.	**Carb:**	None
Calories per serving:	141	**Cholesterol per serving:**	63mg
Total fat grams	5g		

Seafood and Fish

Cod with Mushrooms and Green Chilies

10 oz. skinless cod, coarsely cubed
2 tablespoons for oil
5 green chilies, slit down one side and seeded
1 green bell pepper, seeded and finely chopped
6 bay leaves
1 tablespoon onion powder
1 teaspoon dry mustard
2 onions sliced

1 teaspoon ginger pulp (or ground ginger)
1 teaspoon garlic pulp (or garlic powder)
1 teaspoon chili powder (optional)
salt to taste
1 tablespoon lemon juice
4 oz. mushrooms, sliced
1 tablespoon chopped, fresh cilantro leaves
whole cilantro leaves, tomato slices and lemon wedges for garnish

Method:

Rinse the fish, dry with a paper towel and refrigerate. Heat the corn oil in a deep frying pan or wok. Stir fry the green chilies for 1 minute. Remove chilies from the pan and place on a paper towel.
Put the fish cubes into the pan and stir-fry over moderate heat for 2 minutes. Remove the fish and keep with the chilies in a covered dish.
In the remaining, oil, over low heat, fry the bay leaves, green pepper, onion and mustard for 3 minutes. Add the ginger, garlic, chili powder, salt, lemon juice and mushrooms and mix well.
Put the fish and fried green chilies into the pan and mix all the ingredients well. Cover the pan and cook over low heat for 6-8 minutes until the fish is tender. Garnish the fish with fresh cilantro leaves and serve with a side. dish of low-fat yogurt with chopped, fresh mint.

Serves:	4	Saturated fat:	1 g
Preparation time:	20 min.	Protein:	14g
Cooking time:	10- 15 min.	Carb:	7g
Calories per serving:	149	Cholesterol per serving:	27mg
Total fat grams	8g		

Seafood and Fish

Fish Fillets with New Potatoes and Cauliflower

10 oz. skinless trout fillets (you can use any other find of fish)
10 new potatoes or small potatoes
salt to taste
2 tablespoons corn oil
2 medium onions, sliced
½ teaspoon dry mustard
6 bay leaves

1 small cauliflower, cut into florets
3 garlic cloves
½ teaspoon ginger
1 tablespoon chopped, fresh cilantro leaves (for garnish)
1 tablespoon mild curry powder
1 tablespoon lemon juice
paprika for garnish

Method:

Cut the trout fillets into thick slices and set aside. Scrub the potatoes and cut them in half. Boil the potatoes for 15 minutes or until tender. Drain the water. Heat the oil in a wok or deep frying pan. Add the onions, mustard and bay leaves and sauté for 2 minutes. Add the cauliflower, potatoes, garlic, cloves, curry powder and fish. Stir fry for 2 minutes. Cook over low heat until the fish is tender and the vegetables are well cooked. Pour the lemon juice over the fish and garnish with fresh cilantro leaves and sprinkle with paprika.

Serves:	4	Saturated fat:	1g
Preparation time:	25 min.	Protein:	18g
Cooking time:	20-25 min.	Carb:	23g
Calories per serving:	238	Cholesterol per serving:	30mg
Total fat grams	9g		

Seafood and Fish

Baked Fish with Spicy Almond and Coconut Sauce

2 large whole trout, cleaned (or cod fillets)
2 tablespoons lemon juice
2 tablespoons tomato puree
1 tablespoon ground almonds
1 teaspoon ginger pulp (or ginger powder)
1 teaspoon garlic powder
2 teaspoons garam masala
3 tablespoons low-fat, plain yogurt
Salt to taste
½ cup coconut milk
1 tablespoon chopped, fresh cilantro leaves
2 tablespoons corn oil
1 small bay leaf
2 cardamom pods (or ½ teaspoon ground cardamom)
1 ½ inch piece cinnamon stick
Garnish with sliced almonds, lemon wedges and fresh bay leaves

Method:

Rinse the fish and dry with a paper towel. Sprinkle the fish with the lemon juice. In a bowl mix the tomato puree, ground almonds, ginger, garlic, garam masala, yogurt, salt, coconut milk and the fresh cilantro. Pour in ½ cup of water and stir the mixture until smooth.
In a frying pan, heat the oil with the bay leaf, cardamom and cinnamon for 30 seconds. Pour the sauce and bring to a boil. Stir well. Reduce the heat and cook for another 2 minutes. Pour the sauce over the fish.
Preheat the oven to 375 degrees F. Bake the fish with sauce for 10-15 minutes until the fish is thoroughly cooked.
Garnish the fish with sliced almonds, lemon wedges and bay leaves.
Serve with Basmati rice.

Serves:	4	Saturated fat:	2g
Preparation time:	15 min.	Protein:	18g
Cooking time:	15-20 min.	Carb:	6g
Calories per serving:	207	Cholesterol per serving:	54 mg
Total fat grams	12g		

POULTRY

Poultry

Tandoori Chicken

red food coloring (a few drops) for the chicken
1 chicken, about 3 ½ lbs.
2/3 cup low-fat plain yogurt
1 teaspoon ginger pulp
1 teaspoon garlic pulp
1 tablespoon tomato puree
1 teaspoon paprika
2 tablespoons lemon juice
1 ½ teaspoons ground coriander
1 teaspoon garam masala
salt to taste
corn oil for greasing the baking dish
lemon wedges for garnish
Sliced tomatoes and cilantro leaves for garnish

Method:

Skin the chicken and cut it into 8 pieces. Cover with the red food coloring. Using a sharp knife, make 2 deep slashes in each piece without cutting it through. Pour the yogurt into in large bowl. Add the ginger, garlic, tomato puree, paprika, lemon juice, ground coriander, garam masala, salt and 1 cup water. Mix well and pour over the chicken. Refrigerate chicken with sauce and marinate overnight.

When ready to cook, preheat the oven to its highest temperature. Lift the chicken pieces from the sauce, place them on a greased baking dish and put into the hot oven. Cook the chicken for 15 - 18 minutes, checking several times to make sure it is not browning too fast. If burn marks appear on the chicken turn the chicken over and reduce the heat. Poke the chicken meat to see if it is thoroughly cooked and the juices run clear.

Serves:	4	Saturated fat:	1g
Preparation:	15 min.	Protein:	38g
Plus 3 hrs. (at least)		Carb:	10g
for marinating		Cholesterol per serving:	137mg
Cooking time:	15-18 min.		
Calories per serving:	229		
Total fat grams:	5g		

Poultry

Sauces for Tandoori Chicken

Additional recipes for the tandoori sauce:

4 cups (2 lb. Carton) non-fat yogurt
1 tablespoon curry powder
1 tablespoon paprika

1 teaspoon bottled ginger pulp
1 teaspoon garlic pulp

Method:

Mix all the above ingredients. Thoroughly cover the chicken pieces in the tandoori sauce and refrigerate overnight.

More ingredients for the tandoori sauce:

1 tablespoon ground cardamom
1 teaspoon minced onion
2 tablespoons minced cilantro

1 teaspoon ground cumin
salt to taste
2 tablespoons lemon juice
pepper to taste

Method:

These ingredients can also be added to the tandoori sauce for extra flavor.

Poultry

Spicy Chicken with Tomatoes

- 8 oz. skinless, boned chicken
- fresh parsley leaves
- 3 tablespoons fresh fenugreek or basil leaves
- 2 tablespoons of curry powder
- 1 tablespoon sesame seeds
- 1 tablespoon tamarind paste (substitute the juice of 1 lemon)
- salt to taste
- 1 teaspoon ground coriander
- ½ teaspoon ground cumin
- 1 teaspoon ginger pulp
- 1 teaspoon garlic pulp
- 2 teaspoons cane sugar
- 2 tablespoons corn oil
- 1 ½ teaspoons onion powder
- 6 bay leaves
- 6 medium tomatoes, coarsely chopped
- 2 tablespoons fresh cilantro leaves
- 1 fresh green chili, seeded, sliced (optional for garnish)

Method:

Cut the chicken into cubes and set aside. Wash the parsley and cilantro leaves and dry with a paper towel

Grind the sesame seeds and add the tamarind paste, curry powder, salt, cumin, coriander, ginger, garlic and sugar. Mix 2 tablespoons of water into this sauce. Heat the oil and stir-fry the onion powder, chopped basil leaves and bay leaves over moderate heat for 1 minute. Add the tomatoes and spice paste. Mix everything well and then add the chicken pieces. Stir-fry for 2 minutes. Lower the heat, add the lemon juice and cook for 10 minutes, stirring occasionally. Remove the lid and stir In one tablespoon of the cilantro leaves. Cook for 2 minutes. Serve hot garnished with the remaining cilantro and green chilies. Serve with boiled Basmati rice.

Serves:	4	Saturated fat:	2g
Preparation time:	25 min.	Protein:	15g
Cooking time:	20 min.	Carb:	10g
Calories per serving:	194	Cholesterol per serving:	51g.
Total fat grams:	11g		

Poultry

Chicken with Mango Sauce

2 skinless boned chicken breasts
1 tablespoon olive oil
2 tablespoons lemon juice
Salt to taste

1 tablespoon finely chopped fresh cilantro leaves for garnish
1 red pepper, thinly sliced for garnish

For the Mango Sauce:

2 tablespoons sunflower oil
1 teaspoon onion powder
6 bay leaves
3 tomatoes sliced
1 teaspoon ginger pulp

1 teaspoon garlic pulp
2 tablespoons mango chutney
Salt to taste
1 tablespoon chopped, fresh cilantro leaves

Method:

Rinse the chicken breasts and dry with a paper towel. Using a sharp knife, make 2 slits on each chicken breast to let the spices flavor the meat. In a bowl mix the olive oil, lemon juice and a pinch of salt. Using a pastry brush coat the chicken with this mixture and place in the refrigerator.

To make the mango sauce, heat the sunflower oil in a wok or deep frying pan over moderate heat. Add the onion and bay leaves and stir-fry for 30 seconds. Add the sliced tomato and stir fry for 2 minutes. Add the ginger, garlic, mango chutney, salt and cilantro leaves. Stir-fry for 3 minutes. Add the sour cream and remove from heat. Keep warm. Preheat the broiler and broil the chicken breasts for 4 minutes on each side, until golden brown, basting occasionally. Serve the chicken breasts with the sauce poured on and garnish with cilantro leaves and red pepper strips. (or you can bake the chicken at 375 degrees F for 10 - 15 minutes until the meat is tender).

Serves:	4	Saturated fat:	2g
Preparation time:	20 min.	Protein:	13g
Cooking time:	15 min.	Carb:	6g
Calories per serving:	174	Cholesterol per serving:	35mg
Total fat grams	11g		

Poultry

Lemon and Ginger Chicken

8 oz. skinless, boned chicken pieces
1 ½ cups low-fat plain yogurt
2 tablespoons ginger pulp
1 ½ teaspoons ground coriander
½ teaspoon turmeric
1 teaspoon curry powder
salt to taste
1 tablespoon corn oil
1 bay leaf

10 red and black peppercorns
1 teaspoon ground cardamom seeds
1 tablespoon chopped, fresh cilantro

For the garnish:
Fresh cilantro leaves
8 cherry tomatoes, halved
1 tablespoon shredded ginger

Method:

Cut the chicken into cubes and set aside. In a bowl, mix together the yogurt, lemon juice, ginger, ground coriander and salt. In a frying pan, heat the corn oil with the bay leaf, peppercorns and ground cardamom over a moderate heat, for 2 minutes. Pour in the yogurt and spice mixture and cook for about 1 minute.

Add the chicken. Lower the heat, and cook for 10 minutes until the chicken is cooked through and lightly browned. Stir often to ensure that nothing sticks to the bottom of the pan. Add the cilantro and stir over low heat for 2 minutes.

Put the chicken and sauce on a serving dish and garnish with cilantro leaves, cherry tomatoes and shredded ginger. Serve hot with boiled Basmati rice or rice with coconut.

Serves:	4	Saturated fat:	2 g
Preparation time:	20 min.	Protein:	18 g
Cooking time:	15-20 min.	Carb:	7 g
Calories per serving:	127	Cholesterol per serving:	48mg
Total fat grams	4g		

Poultry

Stir-Fry Chicken with Vegetables

6 oz. boneless chicken
2 tablespoons corn oil
1 teaspoon garlic pulp
1 teaspoon ginger pulp
1 teaspoon mild curry powder
1 teaspoon ground coriander
salt to taste
1 leek sliced
10 medium sized mushrooms thickly sliced

½ green bell pepper, seeded and coarsely chopped
½ red bell pepper, seeded and coarsely chopped
2 tablespoons chopped fresh cilantro leaves
1 tablespoon white sesame seeds
1 tablespoon lemon juice

Method:

Cut the chicken into small pieces. In a bowl combine the oil, garlic, ginger, curry powder, ground coriander and salt. Pour into a wok or deep frying pan and stir-fry over moderate heat for 30 seconds. Add the chicken pieces and mix everything well. Continue stir-frying over moderate heat for 5 minutes. Add the leek, mushrooms, red and green peppers and half the cilantro leaves. Stir fry for another 5 minutes until the chicken is tender. Just before serving, add the sesame seeds and sprinkle the lemon juice over the dish. Garnish with the remaining fresh cilantro leaves.

Serves:	4	Saturated fat:	1 g
Preparation time:	15 min.	Protein:	13 g
Cooking time:	10 min.	Carb:	3 g
Calories per serving:	113	Cholesterol per serving:	31mg
Total fat grams	6g		

Poultry

Chicken with Spicy Sauce

- 4 chicken breast fillets, skinned
- 1 tablespoon tomato puree
- 3 tablespoons low-fat, plain yogurt
- 1 teaspoon garlic pulp
- 1 teaspoon garam masala
- ¼ teaspoon ground cardamom seeds
- 4 tablespoons low-fat ricotta cheese
- 1 teaspoon curry powder
- 1 teaspoon ground almonds
- 1 tablespoon lemon juice
- salt to taste
- 1 tablespoon corn oil
- 1 bay leaf
- 1 cinnamon stick
- 2 tablespoons golden raisins
- 1 tablespoon sliced almonds

Method:

Using a sharp knife, make 2 slashes into each chicken breasts but do <u>not</u> cut through the breast. Place the chicken in a greased baking dish. In a bowl blend together the tomato puree, yogurt, garlic, garam masala, fennel, curry powder, cardamom, ricotta cheese, ground almonds, lemon juice and salt with 4 tablespoons of water. Heat the oil in a deep frying pan. Add the bay leaf and cinnamon stick and fry for 30 seconds. Add the sauce mixture with 2/3 cup water and bring to a boil. Pour the sauce on the chicken breasts and marinate for 1 hour. Preheat the oven to 375 degrees F. Sprinkle the raisins and almonds over the chicken. Cook in the preheated oven for 15-20 minutes until the chicken is firm but thoroughly cooked.

Serves:	4	Saturated fat:	2 g
Preparation time:	15 min.	Protein:	22 g
Cooking time:	20-25 min	Carb:	8 g
Plus 1 hr. marinating		Cholesterol per serving:	56mg
Calories per serving:	217		
Total fat grams	11g		

Poultry

Baked Coconut Chicken

1 chicken about 3 ½ lbs.
1 ½ tablespoons olive oil
1 onion, diced
1 bay leaf
2 cloves
1 inch piece cinnamon stick
3 garlic cloves, crushed
1 teaspoon shredded ginger

7 tablespoons coconut milk
1 teaspoon curry powder
1 teaspoon sugar (optional)
1 teaspoon lemon juice
salt to taste
1 tablespoon fresh cilantro leaves chopped
2 tablespoons golden raisins
1 ½ tablespoons chopped cashew nuts

Method:

Preheat the oven to 375 degrees F. Skin the chicken and cut it into 8 pieces.
Heat the oil in a wok or deep frying pan over moderate heat. Add the onion, bay leaf, cloves, cinnamon, garlic, ginger, 3 tablespoons of the coconut milk, sugar, curry powder, lemon juice, 2/3 cup water and salt to taste. Cook for 2-4 minutes. Add the cilantro, cashew nuts and golden raisins. Stir-fry for 2 minutes over low heat. Add the chicken pieces and the remaining coconut milk. Place the chicken with all the ingredients into a greased baking dish and cook in the oven for 35-40 minutes until the chicken is thoroughly cooked and the meat is tender. Serve hot with boiled Basmati rice.

Serves:	4	Saturated fat:	6 g
Preparation time:	30 min.	Protein:	56g
Cooking time:	40-45 min.	Carb:	30 g
Calories per serving:	350	Cholesterol per serving:	201mg
Total fat grams	25g		

Poultry

Chicken with Rice

- 2 cups Basmati rice
- 1 cinnamon stick
- 2 black cardamom pods
- ½ teaspoon colored peppercorns
- 3 tablespoons chopped fresh cilantro leaves
- salt to taste
- 1 tablespoon olive oil
- 2 tablespoons corn oil
- 1 onion, sliced
- 1 ½ teaspoons ginger pulp
- 1 teaspoon garlic pulp
- 1 teaspoon chili powder (optional)
- 1 ½ teaspoons garam masala
- 1 tablespoon ground almonds
- 2 coconut milk
- 8 oz. skinless boned chicken strips
- 3 tablespoons lemon juice
- 2 oz. shelled peas
- 2 oz. corn kernels
- 1 red pepper, seeded and sliced
- 1 large tomato sliced
- whole cilantro leaves for garnish

Method:

Rinse the rice until the water runs clear. Place the rice in a saucepan with the cinnamon, cardamom, peppercorns and 1 tablespoon of the cilantro. Add 3 cups of water, salt to taste and the olive oil. Bring to a boil over high heat. Lower the heat. Stir the rice gently, and cover with a lid; Cook for 15-20 minutes until the rice is tender. Remove from the heat and set aside.
In a wok or deep frying pan, heat the corn oil. Add the onions and fry over moderate heat, until golden brown. Reduce the heat and add the ginger, garlic, chili powder, garam masala, ground almonds. Coconut milk and salt to taste. Stir-fry all the ingredients for 2 minutes. Add the chicken pieces and cook for 6 minutes. Stir occasionally. Add the lemon juice, peas, corn and bell pepper and stir-fry for 2 minutes. Add another tablespoon of chopped cilantro leaves. Add the cooked rice to the mixture. Cover the dish with a lid and cook over a low heat for 3-5 minutes. Garnish with the remaining cilantro leaves and tomato slices.

Serves:	4	Saturated Fat:	2g
Preparation time	25 min.	Protein:	20g
Cooking time:	30-35 min.	Carb:	56g
Calories per serving:	422	Cholesterol per serving:	51mg
Total fat grams:	13g		

MEATS

Meats

Chicken Curry over Cauliflower Couscous

3 tablespoons olive oil
2 tablespoons mild curry powder
2 teaspoons crushed garlic
1 ½ lbs. chicken cubed
1 red bell pepper, seeded and diced

1 green bell pepper, seeded and diced
1 tablespoon cider vinegar
½ teaspoon salt
2 cups water
1 large cauliflower

Method:

Heat 2 tablespoons of oil over medium heat in a large saucepan. Add curry powder and garlic. Cook and stir 2 minutes until the garlic is golden brown.

Add chicken and coat meat with the curry powder and garlic mixture. Cook over moderate heat for 7 minutes, stirring occasionally. Add bell peppers and vinegar. Cook and stir for 3 minutes until the peppers are soft. Sprinkle with salt.

Add water and bring to a boil. Reduce heat and simmer 30 to 45 minutes stirring occasionally, until the liquid is reduced and chicken is tender, adding water as needed.

Meanwhile trim and core cauliflower. Cut into equal pieces and place in food processor with a metal blade. Process using the on/off pulsing action until the cauliflower is in small, uniform pieces about the size of cooked couscous. Do not puree.

Heat remaining 1 tablespoon oil over medium heat in 12 inch nonstick skillet. Add cauliflower. Cook and stir 5 minutes until the cauliflower is cooked. Do not overcook. Serve chicken curry over cauliflower.

Serves:	4	Saturated fat:	1 g
Preparation time:	5 min.	Protein:	14 g
Cooking time:	15-17 min.	Carb:	2 g
Calories per serving:	113	Cholesterol per serving:	31mg
Total fat grams	5g		

Meats

Shuma's Favorite Ground Turkey Curry Dish

1 lb. 93% fat free ground turkey
1 large Yukon gold potato, thinly sliced
1 large red bell pepper, chopped and seeded
2 bay leaves
1 packet frozen peas
2 tablespoons corn oil

2 tablespoons mild curry powder
2 tablespoons garam masala
1 tablespoon ground cinnamon
1 tablespoon onion powder
salt to taste
2 cups water
cilantro leaves and lemon wedges for garnish

Method:

Heat the oil in a glass lid Dutch oven. Sauté the curry powder, garam masala, cinnamon, onion powder and bay leaves for 1 minute. Add the meat and mix thoroughly with the sautéed ingredients. Brown the meat over moderate heat. Add the potatoes and peppers. Add the water and cook for 5 minutes stirring occasionally. Put some more water, if necessary and boil for 5 minutes. Add salt to taste and garnish with cilantro leaves and lemon wedges.

Serves:	4	Saturated fat:	1g
Preparation time:	5 min.	Protein:	14g
Cooking time:	15 min.	Carb:	4g
Calories per serving:	115	Cholesterol per serving:	28mg
Total fat grams	5g		

Meats

Lamb Patties with Green Spices

1 lb. lean ground lamb or turkey
4 scallions, chopped
2 tablespoon chopped, fresh cilantro leaves
1 tablespoon chopped, fresh mint plus more mint leaves for garnish
2 fresh green chilies, seeded and sliced for garnish

1 teaspoon shredded ginger
1 teaspoon garlic pulp
salt to taste
1 egg, lightly beaten
3 tablespoons corn oil
parsley leaves for garnish

Method:

Mix the ground meat with the scallions, cilantro, mint, ginger, garlic and salt. Stir the ingredients well. Blend in the egg into the mixture. Break off small balls of the mixture and make them into 16 flat, round patties in your palm. When all the patties are made, heat half the oil in a nonstick frying pan over moderate heat. Add half the patties and fry slowly, turning twice and pressing them down as they cook until well-browned for 6-8 minutes. As the patties are cooked remove them from the pan and drain on paper towels to absorb any excess oil.
Cook the remaining patties in the same way and serve hot, garnished with cilantro and mint leaves.

Serves:	4	Saturated fat:	6g
Preparation time:	30 min.	Protein:	25g
Cooking time:	15-20 min.	Carb:	1 g
Calories per serving:	269	Cholesterol per serving:	141mg
Total fat:	18g		

Meats

Lamb or Turkey with Rice

1 lb. lean lamb or turkey cut into thin strips
1 ½ cups low-fat plain yogurt
2 tablespoons ground almonds
¼ teaspoon ground cardamom seeds
1 teaspoon mild curry powder
1 teaspoon garam masala
1 teaspoon ginger pulp
1 teaspoon garlic pulp
1 tablespoon shredded coconut
3 tablespoons chopped, fresh cilantro
4 tablespoons corn oil
2 medium onions sliced
2 oz fresh cut green beans
2 fresh tomatoes, chopped
2 bay leaves
2 cups Basmati rice, washed
3 tablespoons lemon juice
A few slices of green and red bell peppers for garnish

Method:

Place the meat in a large bowl and add the yogurt, ground almonds, cardamom, curry powder, garam masala, ginger, garlic, coconut and 1 tablespoon of the cilantro. Blend everything together and refrigerate overnight.

Heat the oil in a large saucepan over moderate heat. Add the onions, and fry until golden brown. Add the beans, tomatoes, bay leaves and meat mixture. Lower the heat and cook covered for 10 minutes, stirring occasionally.

Pour in the rice and add the cilantro and lemon juice. Pour in 4 cups of water and bring to a boil. Lower the heat, cover with a lid and cook for 15 minutes until the water is absorbed and the rice is cooked. Let the dish stand off the heat for 5 minutes before serving.

Serves:	4	Saturated fat:	9g
Preparation time:	30 min.	Protein:	32g
Cooking time:	45 min.	Carb:	59g
plus 5 min. standing		Cholesterol per serving:	85g
Calories per serving:	592		
Total fat grams	27g		

Meats

Stir-Fry Lamb or Turkey with Pineapple and Peppers

8 oz. boneless lamb or turkey
1 teaspoon ground coriander
1 teaspoon ground cumin
2 teaspoons mango pulp
½ cup plain pineapple juice (without sugar)
1 teaspoon curry powder
1 teaspoon garlic pulp
1 teaspoon ginger pulp
¼ turmeric powder
salt to taste
2 tablespoons corn oil
½ red bell pepper, seeded and cubed
½ green bell pepper, seeded and cubed
12 pineapple chunks (do not add juice or syrup)
1 tablespoon sesame seeds
1 tablespoon fresh cilantro leaves, chopped and whole leaves for garnish

Method:

Cut the meat into small, thin strips and place in a mixing bowl. Add the ground coriander, cumin, curry powder, turmeric and salt. Blend everything thoroughly and refrigerate for 30 minutes.
Heat the oil over moderate heat in a wok or deep frying pan. Drop the meat into the oil and stir-fry for 3 minutes. Add 2/3 cup water and bring to a simmer. Lower the heat, cover the pan and cook for 10 minutes, stirring occasionally. Add the green and red bell pepper pieces, pineapple chunks and chopped cilantro leaves. Stir fry for 2 minutes. Garnish with whole cilantro leaves and sesame seeds.

Serves:	4	Saturated fat:	3g
Preparation time:	20 min.	Protein:	13g
Plus 30 min. marinating		Carb:	10g
Cooking time:	20 min.	Cholesterol per serving:	42mg
Calories per serving:	203		
Total fat grams	13g		

DESSERTS

Desserts

Indian Rice Pudding

½ cup Basmati rice, well rinsed
5 cups low-fat milk
8 tablespoons of sugar
2 tablespoons of shredded coconut

½ teaspoon ground cardamom seeds
½ cup slivered almonds
½ cup golden raisins
pistachio nut for garnish

Method:

Put the washed rice in a deep saucepan. Pour in half the milk and bring to a boil over moderate heat. Continue for 15 minutes over low heat until the rice is cooked. Stir occasionally. Remove from heat. Mash the rice into the milk with a wooden spoon or in a food processor. Add the coconut, cardamom, almonds and raisins. Add the remaining milk to the mixture, return to the heat and cook for 3 minutes over moderate heat, stirring occasionally. Stir in the sugar and cook for 2 minutes. Decorate with shredded coconut and pistachio nuts. Serve cold.

Serves:	4	Saturated fat:	7g
Preparation time:	5 min.	Protein:	12g
Cooking time:	20 min.	Carb:	50g
Calories per serving:	400	Cholesterol per serving:	22mg
Total fat grams	15g		

Desserts

Mango Pulp with Milk

4 large, ripe mangos
1 1/4 cups low-fat milk
½ cup low-fat ricotta cheese
¼ teaspoon nutmeg

¼ teaspoon cinnamon
1 tablespoon sugar
pistachio nuts for garnish

Method:

Remove the pulp from the mangos and discard the pit and the skin
Place the mango pulp in a food processor with the milk, ricotta cheese and sugar. Add the nutmeg and cinnamon. Process until the mixture is smooth.
Transfer to a serving bowl and garnish with pistachio nuts. Serve cold.

Serves:	4	Saturated fat:	3g
Preparation time:	15 min.	Protein:	6 g
Cooking time:	15 min.	Carb:	31g
Calories per serving:	193	Cholesterol per serving	13mg
Total fat grams	6g		

www.ingramcontent.com/pod-product-compliance
Lightning Source LLC
Chambersburg PA
CBHW080349170426
43194CB00014B/2739